GOD, Coffee & Me

Morning Prayer Journal with Scripture

These are the verses you will find this this journal

Genesis 1:16

Psalm 9.1

Romans 8:31

Psalm 3.5

John 5:6

Job 11:18

Lamentations 3:22

2 Corinthians 4:16

1 Peter 2:9

Psalm 31:24

Revelation 21:4

Proverbs 24:20

Romans 15:13

Zephaniah 3:17

Psalm 19:1

Isaiah 41:10

Philippians 4:13

1 Corinthians 10:13

Romans 10:13

Matthew 5:9

1 Peter 5:6

1 Thessalonians 5:11

Psalms 16:8

Isaiah 40:31

Joshua 1:9

Proverbs 18:10

2 Corinthians 1:3

Psalms 46:1

John 14:27

2 Timothy 1:7

Luke 1:14

Psalms 55:22

Isaiah 26:3

Jeremiah 29:11

Genesis 8:1

Proverbs 17:17

1 Corinthians 15:58

Psalms 118:14

Job 13:15

Isaiah 1:19

John 15:13

Proverbs 3:5

Philippians 3:7

Psalm 27:4

Ephesians 3:17

1 John 3:1

Hebrews 10:22

James 1:4

Psalm 23:1

Nahum 1:7

Mark 1:35

Proverbs 15:1

Galatians 6:9

Psalms 119:114

Ephesians 2:10

Colossians 3:2

Philippians 2:3

Matthew 6:33

Psalm 92:1

Isaiah 43:2

1 Corinthians 9:24

Matthew 19:26

Galatians 5:22

Psalm 5:3

Romans 5:3

Titus 2:13

Isaiah 11:9

Psalm 37:4

Daniel 12:3

Philippians 1:6

2 Corinthians 12:9

Numbers 23:19

Psalm 90:17

Hebrews 11:1

1 Corinthians 16:13

Romans 1:16

Acts 15:11

Titus 1:2

Psalm 139:17

James 4:6

Exodus 14:13

Psalm 95:7

Romans 15:13

Hebrews 13:8

Judges 5:31

Ecclesiastes 11:7

Psalm 86:5

Isaiah 50:4

Romans 12:12

1 Timothy 4:10

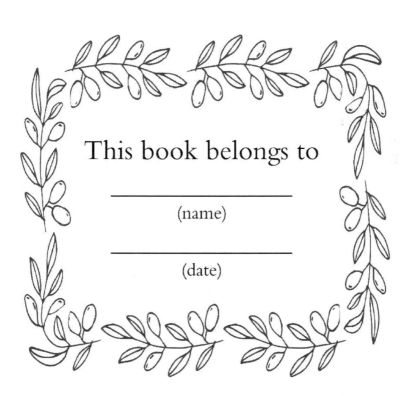

This book belongs to

_____
(name)

_____
(date)

"And God made two great lights; the greater light to rule the day, and the lesser light to rule the night: he made the stars also."
-Genesis 1:16

Have you read the entire chapter in the bible?
Genesis 1:1 – 1:31

☐

Check when you have.

What does this chapter mean to you?

_____
_____
_____
_____
_____

How will you use this message today?

_____
_____
_____
_____
_____

Today's prayer request.

_____
_____
_____

"I will praise thee, O LORD, with my whole heart; I will shew forth all thy marvellous works."
-Psalm 9.1

Have you read the entire chapter in the bible?
Psalms 9.1 – 9:20

Check when you have.

What does this chapter mean to you?

_____

_____

_____

_____

How will you use this message today?

_____

_____

_____

_____

Today's prayer request.

_____

_____

_____

"What shall we then say to these things? If God be for us, who can be against us?"
-Romans 8:31

Have you read the entire chapter in the bible?
Romans 8:1 – 8:39

Check when you have.

What does this chapter mean to you?

_____
_____
_____
_____

How will you use this message today?

_____
_____
_____
_____

Today's prayer request.

_____
_____
_____

> *"I laid me down and slept; I awaked; for the LORD sustained me."*
> -Psalm 3.5

Have you read the entire chapter in the bible?
Psalms 3:1 – 3:8

☐

Check when you have.

What does this chapter mean to you?

_____

_____

_____

_____

_____

How will you use this message today?

_____

_____

_____

_____

_____

Today's prayer request.

_____

_____

_____

> *"When Jesus saw him lie, and knew that he had been now a long time in that case, he saith unto him, Wilt thou be made whole?"*
> -John 5:6

Have you read the entire chapter in the bible?
John 5:1 – 5:37

☐

Check when you have.

What does this chapter mean to you?

_____
_____
_____
_____
_____

How will you use this message today?

_____
_____
_____
_____
_____

Today's prayer request.

_____
_____
_____

"And thou shalt be secure, because there is hope; yea, thou shalt dig about thee, and thou shalt take thy rest in safety."
-Job 11:18

Have you read the entire chapter in the bible?
Job 11:1 – 11:20

☐

Check when you have.

What does this chapter mean to you?

_____
_____
_____
_____

How will you use this message today?

_____
_____
_____
_____

Today's prayer request.

_____
_____
_____

"It is of the LORD's mercies that we are not consumed, because his compassions fail not."
-Lamentations 3:22

Have you read the entire chapter in the bible?
Lamentations 3:1 – 3:66

Check when you have.

What does this chapter mean to you?

_____
_____
_____
_____
_____

How will you use this message today?

_____
_____
_____
_____
_____

Today's prayer request.

_____
_____
_____

"For which cause we faint not; but though our outward man perish, yet the inward man is renewed day by day."

-2 Corinthians 4:16

Have you read the entire chapter in the bible?
2 Corinthians 4:1 – 4:18

☐

Check when you have.

What does this chapter mean to you?

_____
_____
_____
_____
_____

How will you use this message today?

_____
_____
_____
_____
_____

Today's prayer request.

_____
_____
_____

"...that ye should shew forth the praises of him who hath called you out of darkness into his marvellous light...
-1 Peter 2:9

Have you read the entire chapter in the bible?
1 Peter 2:1 – 2:25

☐

Check when you have.

What does this chapter mean to you?

_____
_____
_____
_____
_____

How will you use this message today?

_____
_____
_____
_____
_____

Today's prayer request.

_____
_____
_____

"Be of good courage, and he shall strengthen your heart, all ye that hope in the LORD."
-Psalm 31:24

Have you read the entire chapter in the bible?
Psalms 31:1 – 31:24

Check when you have.

What does this chapter mean to you?

_____
_____
_____
_____
_____

How will you use this message today?

_____
_____
_____
_____
_____

Today's prayer request.

_____
_____
_____

"And God shall wipe away all tears from their eyes; and there shall be no more death, neither sorrow, nor crying..."
-Revelation 21:4

Have you read the entire chapter in the bible?
Revelation 21:1 – 21:27

☐

Check when you have.

What does this chapter mean to you?

_____
_____
_____
_____
_____

How will you use this message today?

_____
_____
_____
_____
_____

Today's prayer request.

_____
_____
_____

> *"For there shall be no reward to the evil man; the candle of the wicked shall be put out."*
> –Proverbs 24:20

Have you read the entire chapter in the bible? **Proverbs 24:1 – 24:20**

Check when you have.

What does this chapter mean to you?

_____
_____
_____
_____
_____

How will you use this message today?

_____
_____
_____
_____
_____

Today's prayer request.

_____
_____
_____

"Now the God of hope fill you with all joy and peace in believing, that ye may abound in hope, through the power of the Holy Ghost."
-Romans 15:13

Have you read the entire chapter in the bible?
Romans 15:1 – 15:33

Check when you have.

What does this chapter mean to you?

_____

_____

_____

_____

How will you use this message today?

_____

_____

_____

_____

_____

Today's prayer request.

_____

_____

_____

"The LORD thy God in the midst of thee is mighty; he will save, he will rejoice over thee with joy..."
–Zephaniah 3:17

Have you read the entire chapter in the bible?
Zephaniah 3:1 – 3:20

☐

Check when you have.

What does this chapter mean to you?

_____
_____
_____
_____
_____

How will you use this message today?

_____
_____
_____
_____
_____

Today's prayer request.

_____
_____
_____

"The heavens declare the glory of God; and the firmament sheweth his handywork."
-Psalm 19:1

Have you read the entire chapter in the bible?
Psalms 19:1 – 19:14

Check when you have.

What does this chapter mean to you?

_____
_____
_____
_____
_____

How will you use this message today?

_____
_____
_____
_____
_____

Today's prayer request.

_____
_____
_____

"Fear thou not; for I am with thee: be not dismayed; for I am thy God: I will strengthen thee; yea..."
-Isaiah 41:10

Have you read the entire chapter in the bible?
Isaiah 41:1 – 41:29

Check when you have.

What does this chapter mean to you?

_____
_____
_____
_____
_____

How will you use this message today?

_____
_____
_____
_____
_____

Today's prayer request.

_____
_____
_____

"I can do all things through Christ which strengtheneth me."
-Philippians 4:13

Have you read the entire chapter in the bible?
Philippians 4:1 – 4:23

☐

Check when you have.

What does this chapter mean to you?

_____
_____
_____
_____
_____

How will you use this message today?

_____
_____
_____
_____
_____

Today's prayer request.

_____
_____
_____

"There hath no temptation taken you but such as is common to man: but God is faithful..."
-1 Corinthians 10:13

Have you read the entire chapter in the bible?
1 Corinthians 10:1 – 10:33

☐

Check when you have.

What does this chapter mean to you?

_____
_____
_____
_____

How will you use this message today?

_____
_____
_____
_____
_____

Today's prayer request.

_____
_____
_____

"For whosoever shall call upon the name of the Lord shall be saved."
-Romans 10:13

Have you read the entire chapter in the bible?
Romans 10:1 – 10:21

Check when you have.

What does this chapter mean to you?

_____
_____
_____
_____

How will you use this message today?

_____
_____
_____
_____

Today's prayer request.

_____
_____
_____

"Blessed are the peacemakers: for they shall be called the children of God. "

-Matthew 5:9

Have you read the entire chapter in the bible?
Matthew 5:1 – 5:48

Check when you have.

What does this chapter mean to you?

_____
_____
_____
_____
_____

How will you use this message today?

_____
_____
_____
_____
_____

Today's prayer request.

_____
_____
_____

"Humble yourselves therefore under the mighty hand of God, that he may exalt you in due time..."
-1 Peter 5:6

Have you read the entire chapter in the bible?
1 Peter 5:1 – 5:14

☐

Check when you have.

What does this chapter mean to you?

_____
_____
_____
_____
_____

How will you use this message today?

_____
_____
_____
_____
_____

Today's prayer request.

_____
_____
_____

"Wherefore comfort yourselves together, and edify one another, even as also ye do."
-1 Thessalonians 5:11

Have you read the entire chapter in the bible? *Thessalonians 5:1 – 5:28*

Check when you have.

What does this chapter mean to you?

_____
_____
_____
_____
_____

How will you use this message today?

_____
_____
_____
_____
_____

Today's prayer request.

_____
_____
_____

"I have set the LORD always before me: because he is at my right hand, I shall not be moved."
-Psalms 16:8

Have you read the entire chapter in the bible?
Psalms 16:1 – 16:11

Check when you have.

What does this chapter mean to you?

_____
_____
_____
_____
_____

How will you use this message today?

_____
_____
_____
_____
_____

Today's prayer request.

_____
_____
_____

"But they that wait upon the LORD shall renew their strength; they shall mount up with wings as eagles..."
-Isaiah 40:31

Have you read the entire chapter in the bible?
Isaiah 40:1 – 40:31

☐

Check when you have.

What does this chapter mean to you?

_____
_____
_____
_____
_____

How will you use this message today?

_____
_____
_____
_____
_____

Today's prayer request.

_____
_____
_____

"...be not afraid, neither be thou dismayed: for the LORD thy God is with thee whithersoever thou goest."
-Joshua 1:9

Have you read the entire chapter in the bible?
Joshua 1:1 – 1:18

Check when you have.

What does this chapter mean to you?

_____
_____
_____
_____
_____

How will you use this message today?

_____
_____
_____
_____
_____

Today's prayer request.

_____
_____
_____

"The name of the LORD is a strong tower: the righteous runneth into it, and is safe."
-Proverbs 18:10

Have you read the entire chapter in the bible?
Proverbs 18:1 – 18:24

Check when you have.

What does this chapter mean to you?

_____
_____
_____
_____
_____

How will you use this message today?

_____
_____
_____
_____
_____

Today's prayer request.

_____
_____
_____

"Blessed be God, even the Father of our Lord Jesus Christ, the Father of mercies, and the God of all comfort..."
-2 Corinthians 1:3

Have you read the entire chapter in the bible?
2 Corinthians 1:1 – 1:24

Check when you have.

What does this chapter mean to you?

_____
_____
_____
_____
_____

How will you use this message today?

_____
_____
_____
_____
_____

Today's prayer request.

_____
_____
_____

> *"God is our refuge and strength, a very present help in trouble."*
> -Psalms 46:1

Have you read the entire chapter in the bible?
Psalms 46:1 – 46:41

☐

Check when you have.

What does this chapter mean to you?

_____
_____
_____
_____
_____

How will you use this message today?

_____
_____
_____
_____
_____

Today's prayer request.

_____
_____
_____

"Peace I leave with you, my peace I give unto you: not as the world giveth, give I unto you."
–John 14:27

Have you read the entire chapter in the bible?
John 14:1 – 14:31

Check when you have.

What does this chapter mean to you?

_____
_____
_____
_____
_____

How will you use this message today?

_____
_____
_____
_____
_____

Today's prayer request.

_____
_____
_____

"For God hath not given us the spirit of fear; but of power, and of love, and of a sound mind."
-2 Timothy 1:7

Have you read the entire chapter in the bible?
2 Timothy 1:1 – 1:18

Check when you have.

What does this chapter mean to you?

_____
_____
_____
_____
_____

How will you use this message today?

_____
_____
_____
_____
_____

Today's prayer request.

_____
_____
_____

"You will have joy and gladness, and many will rejoice at his birth."
-Luke 1:14

Have you read the entire chapter in the bible?
Luke 1:1 – 1:80

Check when you have.

What does this chapter mean to you?

_____
_____
_____
_____
_____

How will you use this message today?

_____
_____
_____
_____
_____

Today's prayer request.

_____
_____
_____

"Cast thy burden upon the LORD, and he shall sustain thee: he shall never suffer the righteous to be moved."
-Psalms 55:22

Have you read the entire chapter in the bible?
Psalms 55-1 – 55:23

Check when you have.

What does this chapter mean to you?

_____
_____
_____
_____
_____

How will you use this message today?

_____
_____
_____
_____
_____

Today's prayer request.

_____
_____
_____

"Thou wilt keep him in perfect peace, whose mind is stayed on thee: because he trusteth in thee."
-Isaiah 26:3

Have you read the entire chapter in the bible? *Isaiah 26:1 – 26:1*

☐

Check when you have.

What does this chapter mean to you?

_____
_____
_____
_____
_____

How will you use this message today?

_____
_____
_____
_____
_____

Today's prayer request.

_____
_____
_____

"For I know the thoughts that I think toward you, saith the LORD, thoughts of peace, and not of evil, to give you an expected end."
-Jeremiah 29:11

Have you read the entire chapter in the bible?
Jeremiah 1:29 – 1:32

☐

Check when you have.

What does this chapter mean to you?

_____
_____
_____
_____
_____

How will you use this message today?

_____
_____
_____
_____
_____

Today's prayer request.

_____
_____
_____

"And God remembered Noah, and every living thing, and all the cattle that was with him in the ark:..."
-Genesis 8:1

Have you read the entire chapter in the bible? **Genesis 8:1 – 8:22**

Check when you have.

What does this chapter mean to you?

_____
_____
_____
_____
_____

How will you use this message today?

_____
_____
_____
_____
_____

Today's prayer request.

_____
_____
_____

"A friend loveth at all times, and a brother is born for adversity."
-Proverbs 17:17

Have you read the entire chapter in the bible?
Proverbs 17:1 – 17:28

Check when you have.

What does this chapter mean to you?

_____
_____
_____
_____

How will you use this message today?

_____
_____
_____
_____

Today's prayer request.

_____
_____
_____

"Therefore, my beloved brethren, be ye stedfast, unmoveable, always abounding in the work of the Lord..."
-1 Corinthians 15:58

Have you read the entire chapter in the bible?
1 Corinthians 15:1 – 15:58

☐

Check when you have.

What does this chapter mean to you?

_____
_____
_____
_____

How will you use this message today?

_____
_____
_____
_____

Today's prayer request.

_____
_____
_____

> *"The LORD is my strength and song, and is become my salvation."*
> -Psalms 118:14

Have you read the entire chapter in the bible?
Psalms 118:1 – 118:29

Check when you have.

What does this chapter mean to you?

_____
_____
_____
_____
_____

How will you use this message today?

_____
_____
_____
_____
_____

Today's prayer request.

_____
_____
_____

"Though he slay me, yet will I trust in him: but I will maintain mine own ways before him."
-Job 13:15

Have you read the entire chapter in the bible?
Job 13:1 – 13:28

☐

Check when you have.

What does this chapter mean to you?

_____
_____
_____
_____
_____

How will you use this message today?

_____
_____
_____
_____
_____

Today's prayer request.

_____
_____
_____

"If ye be willing and obedient, ye shall eat the good of the land…"
-Isaiah 1:19

Have you read the entire chapter in the bible? *Isaiah 1:1 – 1:31*

☐

Check when you have.

What does this chapter mean to you?

_____
_____
_____
_____
_____

How will you use this message today?

_____
_____
_____
_____
_____

Today's prayer request.

_____
_____
_____

"Greater love hath no man than this, that a man lay down his life for his friends."
-John 15:13

Have you read the entire chapter in the bible?
John 15:1 – 15:27

Check when you have.

What does this chapter mean to you?

_____
_____
_____
_____
_____

How will you use this message today?

_____
_____
_____
_____
_____

Today's prayer request.

_____
_____
_____

"Trust in the LORD with all thine heart; and lean not unto thine own understanding."
-Proverbs 3:5

Have you read the entire chapter in the bible?
Proverbs 3:1 – 3:35

☐

Check when you have.

What does this chapter mean to you?

_____
_____
_____
_____
_____

How will you use this message today?

_____
_____
_____
_____
_____

Today's prayer request.

_____
_____
_____

"But what things were gain to me, those I counted loss for Christ."
-Philippians 3:7

Have you read the entire chapter in the bible? **Philippians 3:1 – 3:21**

Check when you have.

What does this chapter mean to you?

_____
_____
_____
_____
_____

How will you use this message today?

_____
_____
_____
_____
_____

Today's prayer request.

_____
_____
_____

"One thing have I desired of the LORD, that will I seek after; that I may dwell in the house of the LORD all the days of my life..."
-Psalm 27:4

Have you read the entire chapter in the bible?
Psalms 27:1 – 27:14

☐

Check when you have.

What does this chapter mean to you?

_____
_____
_____
_____
_____

How will you use this message today?

_____
_____
_____
_____
_____

Today's prayer request.

_____
_____
_____

"That Christ may dwell in your hearts by faith; that ye, being rooted and grounded in love..."
-Ephesians 3:17

Have you read the entire chapter in the bible?
Ephesians 3:1 – 3:21

Check when you have.

What does this chapter mean to you?

_____
_____
_____
_____

How will you use this message today?

_____
_____
_____
_____
_____

Today's prayer request.

_____
_____
_____

> *"Behold, what manner of love the Father hath bestowed upon us, that we should be called the sons of God: therefore the world knoweth us not, because it knew him not."*
>
> -1 John 3:1

Have you read the entire chapter in the bible?
1 John 3:1 – 3:36

☐

Check when you have.

What does this chapter mean to you?

_____

_____

_____

_____

How will you use this message today?

_____

_____

_____

_____

Today's prayer request.

_____

_____

_____

"Let us draw near with a true heart in full assurance of faith, having our hearts sprinkled from an evil conscience..."
-Hebrews 10:22

Have you read the entire chapter in the bible?
Hebrews 10:1 – 10:39

Check when you have.

What does this chapter mean to you?

_____
_____
_____
_____
_____

How will you use this message today?

_____
_____
_____
_____
_____

Today's prayer request.

_____
_____
_____

"But let patience have her perfect work, that ye may be perfect and entire, wanting nothing."
-James 1:4

Have you read the entire chapter in the bible?
James 1:1 – 1:27

Check when you have.

What does this chapter mean to you?

_____
_____
_____
_____

How will you use this message today?

_____
_____
_____
_____

Today's prayer request.

_____
_____
_____

"The LORD is my shepherd; I shall not want."
-Psalm 23:1

Have you read the entire chapter in the bible?
Psalms 23:1 – 23:6

Check when you have.

What does this chapter mean to you?

_____
_____
_____
_____

How will you use this message today?

_____
_____
_____
_____

Today's prayer request.

_____
_____
_____

"The LORD is good, a strong hold in the day of trouble; and he knoweth them that trust in him."
-Nahum 1:7

Have you read the entire chapter in the bible?
Nahum 1:1 – 1:15

Check when you have.

What does this chapter mean to you?

_____
_____
_____
_____
_____

How will you use this message today?

_____
_____
_____
_____
_____

Today's prayer request.

_____
_____
_____

"And in the morning, rising up a great while before day, he went out, and departed into a solitary place, and there prayed."
–Mark 1:35

Have you read the entire chapter in the bible?
Mark 1:1 – 1:45

Check when you have.

What does this chapter mean to you?

_____
_____
_____
_____
_____

How will you use this message today?

_____
_____
_____
_____
_____

Today's prayer request.

_____
_____
_____

"A soft answer turneth away wrath: but grievous words stir up anger."
-Proverbs 15:1

Have you read the entire chapter in the bible?
Proverbs 15:1 – 15:33

☐

Check when you have.

What does this chapter mean to you?

_____
_____
_____
_____
_____

How will you use this message today?

_____
_____
_____
_____
_____

Today's prayer request.

_____
_____
_____

"And let us not be weary in well doing: for in due season we shall reap, if we faint not."
-Galatians 6:9

Have you read the entire chapter in the bible? *Galatians 15:1 – 15:18*

Check when you have.

What does this chapter mean to you?

_____
_____
_____
_____
_____

How will you use this message today?

_____
_____
_____
_____
_____

Today's prayer request.

_____
_____
_____

"Thou art my hiding place and my shield: I hope in thy word."
-Psalms 119:114

Have you read the entire chapter in the bible?
Psalms 119:1 – 119:176

Check when you have.

What does this chapter mean to you?

_____

_____

_____

_____

_____

How will you use this message today?

_____

_____

_____

_____

_____

Today's prayer request.

_____

_____

_____

"For we are his workmanship, created in Christ Jesus unto good works, which God hath before ordained that we should walk in them."
-Ephesians 2:10

Have you read the entire chapter in the bible?
Ephesians 2:1 – 2:22

☐

Check when you have.

What does this chapter mean to you?

_____
_____
_____
_____
_____

How will you use this message today?

_____
_____
_____
_____
_____

Today's prayer request.

_____
_____
_____

"Set your affection on things above, not on things on the earth."
-Colossians 3:2

Have you read the entire chapter in the bible?
Colossians 3:2 – 3:25

☐

Check when you have.

What does this chapter mean to you?

_____
_____
_____
_____
_____

How will you use this message today?

_____
_____
_____
_____
_____

Today's prayer request.

_____
_____
_____

"Let nothing be done through strife or vainglory; but in lowliness of mind let each esteem other better than themselves."
-Philippians 2:3

Have you read the entire chapter in the bible?
Philippians 2:1 – 2:30

Check when you have.

What does this chapter mean to you?

_____
_____
_____
_____
_____

How will you use this message today?

_____
_____
_____
_____
_____

Today's prayer request.

_____
_____
_____

"But seek ye first the kingdom of God, and his righteousness; and all these things shall be added unto you."

-Matthew 6:33

Have you read the entire chapter in the bible?
Matthew 6:1 – 6:34

Check when you have.

What does this chapter mean to you?

_____
_____
_____
_____
_____

How will you use this message today?

_____
_____
_____
_____
_____

Today's prayer request.

_____
_____
_____

"It is a good thing to give thanks unto the LORD, and to sing praises unto thy name, O Most High..."
-Psalm 92:1

Have you read the entire chapter in the bible?
Psalms 92:1 – 92:15

Check when you have.

What does this chapter mean to you?

_____
_____
_____
_____

How will you use this message today?

_____
_____
_____
_____
_____

Today's prayer request.

_____
_____
_____

"When thou passest through the waters, I will be with thee; and through the rivers, they shall not overflow thee..."
-Isaiah 43:2

Have you read the entire chapter in the bible?
Isaiah 43:1 – 43:28

Check when you have.

What does this chapter mean to you?

_____
_____
_____
_____
_____

How will you use this message today?

_____
_____
_____
_____
_____

Today's prayer request.

_____
_____
_____

"Know ye not that they which run in a race run all, but one receiveth the prize? So run, that ye may obtain."

-1 Corinthians 9:24

Have you read the entire chapter in the bible?
1 Corinthians 9.1 – 9.27

Check when you have.

What does this chapter mean to you?

_____
_____
_____
_____
_____

How will you use this message today?

_____
_____
_____
_____
_____

Today's prayer request.

_____
_____
_____

"But Jesus beheld them, and said unto them, With men this is impossible; but with God all things are possible."
-Matthew 19:26

Have you read the entire chapter in the bible?
Matthew 19:1 – 19:30

☐

Check when you have.

What does this chapter mean to you?

_____
_____
_____
_____
_____

How will you use this message today?

_____
_____
_____
_____
_____

Today's prayer request.

_____
_____
_____

"But the fruit of the Spirit is love, joy, peace, longsuffering, gentleness, goodness, faith..."
-Galatians 5:22

Have you read the entire chapter in the bible?
Galatians 5:1 – 5:26

Check when you have.

What does this chapter mean to you?

_____
_____
_____
_____
_____

How will you use this message today?

_____
_____
_____
_____
_____

Today's prayer request.

_____
_____
_____

"My voice shalt thou hear in the morning, O LORD; in the morning will I direct my prayer unto thee, and will look up."
-Psalm 5:3

Have you read the entire chapter in the bible?
Psalms 5:1 – 5:12

☐

Check when you have.

What does this chapter mean to you?

_____

_____

_____

_____

How will you use this message today?

_____

_____

_____

_____

Today's prayer request.

_____

_____

_____

"And not only so, but we glory in tribulations also: knowing that tribulation worketh patience..."
-Romans 5:3

Have you read the entire chapter in the bible?
Romans 5:1 – 5:21

☐

Check when you have.

What does this chapter mean to you?

_____
_____
_____
_____
_____

How will you use this message today?

_____
_____
_____
_____
_____

Today's prayer request.

_____
_____
_____

"Looking for that blessed hope, and the glorious appearing of the great God and our Saviour Jesus Christ..."
-Titus 2:13

Have you read the entire chapter in the bible? *Titus 2:1 – 2:15*

Check when you have.

What does this chapter mean to you?

_____
_____
_____
_____
_____

How will you use this message today?

_____
_____
_____
_____
_____

Today's prayer request.

_____
_____
_____

> *"They shall not hurt nor destroy in all my holy mountain: for the earth shall be full of the knowledge of the LORD, as the waters cover the sea."*
> -Isaiah 11:9

Have you read the entire chapter in the bible?
Isaiah 11:1 – 11:16

☐

Check when you have.

What does this chapter mean to you?

_____
_____
_____
_____
_____

How will you use this message today?

_____
_____
_____
_____
_____

Today's prayer request.

_____
_____
_____

"Delight thyself also in the LORD: and he shall give thee the desires of thine heart."
-Psalm 37:4

Have you read the entire chapter in the bible?
Psalms 37:1 – 37:40

☐

Check when you have.

What does this chapter mean to you?

_____

_____

_____

_____

How will you use this message today?

_____

_____

_____

_____

Today's prayer request.

_____

_____

_____

"And they that be wise shall shine as the brightness of the firmament; and they that turn many to righteousness as the stars for ever and ever."
-Daniel 12:3

Have you read the entire chapter in the bible? *Daniel 12:1 – 12:13*

Check when you have.

What does this chapter mean to you?

_____
_____
_____
_____
_____

How will you use this message today?

_____
_____
_____
_____
_____

Today's prayer request.

_____
_____
_____

> *"Being confident of this very thing, that he which hath begun a good work in you will perform it until the day of Jesus Christ...*
> -Philippians 1:6

Have you read the entire chapter in the bible?
Philippians 1:1 – 1:30

☐

Check when you have.

What does this chapter mean to you?

_____

_____

_____

_____

How will you use this message today?

_____

_____

_____

_____

Today's prayer request.

_____

_____

_____

"And he said unto me, My grace is sufficient for thee: for my strength is made perfect in weakness..."
-2 Corinthians 12:9

Have you read the entire chapter in the bible?
2 Corinthians 12:1 – 12:21

Check when you have.

What does this chapter mean to you?

_____
_____
_____
_____
_____

How will you use this message today?

_____
_____
_____
_____
_____

Today's prayer request.

_____
_____
_____

> *"God is not a man, that he should lie; neither the son of man, that he should repent: hath he said, and shall he not do it?"*
> -Numbers 23:19

Have you read the entire chapter in the bible?
Numbers 23:1 – 23:30

☐

Check when you have.

What does this chapter mean to you?

_____
_____
_____
_____
_____

How will you use this message today?

_____
_____
_____
_____
_____

Today's prayer request.

_____
_____
_____

"And let the beauty of the LORD our God be upon us: and establish thou the work of our hands upon us..."
-Psalm 90:17

Have you read the entire chapter in the bible?
Psalms 90:1 – 90:17

[ ]

Check when you have.

What does this chapter mean to you?

_____
_____
_____
_____
_____

How will you use this message today?

_____
_____
_____
_____
_____

Today's prayer request.

_____
_____
_____

"Now faith is the substance of things hoped for, the evidence of things not seen."
-Hebrews 11:1

Have you read the entire chapter in the bible?
Hebrews 11:1 – 11:40

☐

Check when you have.

What does this chapter mean to you?

_____
_____
_____
_____
_____

How will you use this message today?

_____
_____
_____
_____
_____

Today's prayer request.

_____
_____
_____

> *"Watch ye, stand fast in the faith, quit you like men, be strong."*
> -1 Corinthians 16:13

Have you read the entire chapter in the bible?
1 Corinthians 16:1 – 16:24

☐

Check when you have.

What does this chapter mean to you?

_____
_____
_____
_____
_____

How will you use this message today?

_____
_____
_____
_____
_____

Today's prayer request.

_____
_____
_____

"For I am not ashamed of the gospel of Christ: for it is the power of God unto salvation to every one that believeth."
-Romans 1:16

Have you read the entire chapter in the bible?
Romans 1:1 – 1:32

☐

Check when you have.

What does this chapter mean to you?

_____
_____
_____
_____
_____

How will you use this message today?

_____
_____
_____
_____
_____

Today's prayer request.

_____
_____
_____

"But we believe that through the grace of the LORD Jesus Christ we shall be saved, even as they."
-Acts 15:11

Have you read the entire chapter in the bible?
Acts 15:1 – 15:41

Check when you have.

What does this chapter mean to you?

_____
_____
_____
_____
_____

How will you use this message today?

_____
_____
_____
_____
_____

Today's prayer request.

_____
_____
_____

"In hope of eternal life, which God, that cannot lie, promised before the world began..."
-Titus 1:2

Have you read the entire chapter in the bible?
Titus 1:1 – 1:16

☐

Check when you have.

What does this chapter mean to you?

_____
_____
_____
_____
_____

How will you use this message today?

_____
_____
_____
_____
_____

Today's prayer request.

_____
_____
_____

"How precious also are thy thoughts unto me, O God! how great is the sum of them!"
–Psalm 139:17

Have you read the entire chapter in the bible?
Psalms 139:1 – 139:24

Check when you have.

What does this chapter mean to you?

_____
_____
_____
_____
_____

How will you use this message today?

_____
_____
_____
_____
_____

Today's prayer request.

_____
_____
_____

"But he giveth more grace. Wherefore he saith, God resisteth the proud, but giveth grace unto the humble."

–James 4:6

Have you read the entire chapter in the bible?
James 4:1 – 4:17

☐

Check when you have.

What does this chapter mean to you?

_____
_____
_____
_____

How will you use this message today?

_____
_____
_____
_____

Today's prayer request.

_____
_____
_____

"Fear ye not, stand still, and see the salvation of the LORD, which he will shew to you to day..."
-Exodus 14:13

Have you read the entire chapter in the bible?
Exodus 14:1 – 14:31

Check when you have.

What does this chapter mean to you?

_____
_____
_____
_____
_____

How will you use this message today?

_____
_____
_____
_____
_____

Today's prayer request.

_____
_____
_____

"For he is our God; and we are the people of his pasture, and the sheep of his hand. To day if ye will hear his voice..."
-Psalm 95:7

Have you read the entire chapter in the bible?
Psalms 95:1 – 95:11

Check when you have.

What does this chapter mean to you?

_____
_____
_____
_____
_____

How will you use this message today?

_____
_____
_____
_____
_____

Today's prayer request.

_____
_____
_____

> *"The God of my rock; in him will I trust: he is my shield, and the horn of my salvation, my high tower, and my refuge, my saviour; thou savest me from violence."*
>
> -2 Samuel 22:3

Have you read the entire chapter in the bible?
2 Samuel 22:1 – 22:51

Check when you have.

What does this chapter mean to you?

_____
_____
_____
_____
_____

How will you use this message today?

_____
_____
_____
_____
_____

Today's prayer request.

_____
_____
_____

"Jesus Christ the same yesterday, and to day, and for ever."
-Hebrews 13:8

Have you read the entire chapter in the bible?
Hebrews 13:1 – 13:25

☐

Check when you have.

What does this chapter mean to you?

_____
_____
_____
_____
_____

How will you use this message today?

_____
_____
_____
_____
_____

Today's prayer request.

_____
_____
_____

> *"O LORD: but let them that love him be as the sun when he goeth forth in his might."*
> -Judges 5:31

Have you read the entire chapter in the bible? *Judges 5:1 – 5:31*

Check when you have.

What does this chapter mean to you?

_____
_____
_____
_____
_____

How will you use this message today?

_____
_____
_____
_____
_____

Today's prayer request.

_____
_____
_____

"Truly the light is sweet, and a pleasant thing it is for the eyes to behold the sun…"
-Ecclesiastes 11:7

Have you read the entire chapter in the bible?
Ecclesiastes 11:1 – 11:10

☐

Check when you have.

What does this chapter mean to you?

_____

_____

_____

_____

How will you use this message today?

_____

_____

_____

_____

Today's prayer request.

_____

_____

_____

"For thou, Lord, art good, and ready to forgive; and plenteous in mercy unto all them that call upon thee. "
-Psalm 86:5

Have you read the entire chapter in the bible?
Psalms 86:1 – 86:17

Check when you have.

What does this chapter mean to you?

_____
_____
_____
_____
_____

How will you use this message today?

_____
_____
_____
_____
_____

Today's prayer request.

_____
_____
_____

"...he wakeneth morning by morning, he wakeneth mine ear to hear as the learned."
-Isaiah 50:4

Have you read the entire chapter in the bible?
Isaiah 50:1 – 50:11

Check when you have.

What does this chapter mean to you?

_____
_____
_____
_____

How will you use this message today?

_____
_____
_____
_____

Today's prayer request.

_____
_____
_____

"Rejoicing in hope; patient in tribulation; continuing instant in prayer..."
-Romans 12:12

Have you read the entire chapter in the bible?
Romans 12:1 – 12:21

Check when you have.

What does this chapter mean to you?

How will you use this message today?

Today's prayer request.

"For therefore we both labour and suffer reproach, because we trust in the living God, who is the Saviour of all men, specially of those that believe."
1 Timothy 4:10

Have you read the entire chapter in the bible?
1 Timothy 4:1 – 4:16

☐

Check when you have.

What does this chapter mean to you?

_____
_____
_____
_____
_____

How will you use this message today?

_____
_____
_____
_____
_____

Today's prayer request.

_____
_____
_____

Notes

Notes

Notes

Notes

Notes

Notes

Notes

Notes

Notes

Notes

Notes

Notes

More journals you might like from...

Add your thoughts, reflections and prayers
in this beautiful journal. Find it at Amazon
– ISBN # *10: 1983272590*

This beautifully designed gratitude journal holds an entire year's worth of your thanks. Find it at Amazon – ISBN # *10: 1983086827*

Made in the USA
San Bernardino, CA
03 November 2019